GENESIS: ORIGIN OF LOVE

KOMALIKA NEYOL

Made with ♥ on the Notion Press Platform
www.notionpress.com

For Ali

Contents

Prologue

I, 'I', Me, or Myself refers to the writer's self that exists in the physical realm of the world.

i refers to the writer's transcendental self or being that exists beyond the physical realm but is the objective observer of it. It can also be considered as consciousness.

You, 'You', or Yours refers to the reader's self that exists in the physical realm of the world.

you refers to the reader's transcendental self or being that exists beyond the physical realm but is the objective observer of it. It can also be considered as the reader's consciousness.

Energy, Enigmatic Body, God, and Law refer to what is supreme to all the contents of the physical realm, and the consciousness of the writer and the reader. It is the unifying force that sets all kinds of being in motion and is also the reason for its cessation.

Being refers to the act in which the subject can just be. However, It is independent of the act itself.

One and Uncountable is the concept borrowed from the Sufi tradition where God is referred to as one but he and his oneness are uncountable.

Life and Death refer to the events that take place in the physical realm that lead to the origin and the cessation of I, You, and all beings.

life and death are metaphors for the indescribable nature of a being's essence. life can also be considered as the metaphor for what nourishes, loves, and brings peace, happiness, and joy. It can be understood as a form in which energy manifests itself. Whereas, death can be considered as the metaphor for what gets nourished, loves, and brings peace, stability, and compassion. It can also be understood as a form in which energy manifests itself more potently.

1. THE STAGE

may you cry the tears of joy,
of love, of compassion, of satisfaction,
when 'I' leave the Stage.
dancing, singing, and sometimes being still,
entertaining you with movement, music, and the loud silence,
when 'I' am in the Act.
it was all anticipation,
in goddess, in grandparents, and in the Lover,
before 'I' set my foot on the Stage.
it doesn't matter who acts, who falls,
who entertains, who gets entertained,
for the only thing that stays is
THE STAGE.

2. You're More Dear to Me than I

you're more dear to me,
than all the words 'I' have ever known
more than the feelings 'I' feel
and the sensations 'I' know
you're close to the Consciousness in
the Being with this body
with Your Being
you and me, we're the Consciousness flowing
from the same Stream
then is there really a separate
'You' and 'Me'?
myself as you as me
is what i've seen
then would that make us 'One'
or the 'Uncountable'?
has ever anyone counted air, water, fire, or matter?

3. Butterflies

you're the Cucoon
to the Butterfly i am
but you're also the Flowers and the Pigment of my Wings
you're the Wind to my Flights
also the Flutter
and the Hurricane caused by my Wings
I wonder if 'You' and 'Me' are the illusions
of the same Energy.

4. Illusion of Separation

You, Me, the Tress, & the Wind
the Wind, the Sky, the Sun, & the Moon
the Moon, the Night, the Daylight, & Us
Us, the God, the Divine, & the Devotees
'We' are all just 'One'.
there's no Separation
No Separate, You, & Me
Them, or They
the 'One' is the 'Uncountable'.

5. Let God Take Me

If I can't be Close to You
let God take away my consciousness and dissolve Me
for everything you will make a Dua
it'll have an essence of me

6. you're so full of life

you're so full of Life
and They call me Death
you're synonymous with Suffering
and i am their Release
i follow you everywhere you go
hang on Your head like a sword of Destruction
yet there's no existence of
me without you

7. be with Me, please?

what do you call it when there's only one person you can think of everywhere you go?

As If, they carry a piece of you, a precious one, an innocent one.

why do I feel the Guilt every time I Think about someone else? why do I want to give You this special place in Me when You are not ready to be Here? be with Me? with Me? You & Me? Please?

8. We Are Meaningless

i'm the Heart of the same Body
you're the Ribcage of
protecting my Being
while i work tirelessly to feed you
with every Pump that sets the Law in Motion
you receive a Drop of the entire Ocean
while there's no meaning of your Being without me
but i'd collapse the moment you Un-Be
so i guess We Are BOTH Meaningless
i guess we're both meaningless
loving each other meaninglessly
the only One we truly serve is this
Enigmatic Body.

9. To Love is to Be in Pain

I paint a picture of Us,
sitting under My favorite tree
You caressing My hair
and My head on Your shoulder
I wiggle My toes,
Then rub My feet across Yours
Feeling the gentleness and warmth of Your skin
Wondering how much You had to suffer to be so soft
You put Your hand on my cheek
Rubbing Your thumb gently under my eye
We lock our gaze into each other
I wonder how can the entire universe be right here
I feel the words Your Heart whispers
I hear the things You never say
Among the noise of rustling dead leaves that surround us
Wondering how long before We speak
I shut my eyes slowly
Feeling the lids getting heavier
But I'm scared to Sleep
Wondering if You'll disappear like a Fever Dream
To Love is to Be in Pain,
sprinkled all over the moments of solitude

the Peace is in Your Thoughts,
the Healing in Your Longing.

10. I write You letters so I don't have any regrets left

touch me somewhere no one has ever touched before, break the walls of my heart and build it into your favorite castle. I write You letters, mostly talking to my own self, just so that i don't have any regrets left.

11. Misfits

you and me,

we're apples of the same tree

we heal by helping others

we unite in the separation

we free ourselves in enslavement

we love with the pain

you and me,

the misfits of the society.

you and me,

we're puppets of the same destiny

you and me,

we live the same tragedy

you and me,

a dream, we wish could be!

12. skiing on the strings of my guitar

You've got more life in yourself than all the stars combined in the sky and yet you question how are you not pure magic?

13. happy birthday, circa 2023

You are like a white swan
with a heart of an angel
a touch of midas
and a mind of nature
oh, the hidden pleasure and the obvious pain!
like a child of poetry
and the father of procreation
a reflection of the divine
and glimpse of devil's rage
oh, the courage and the fears of this man!
the trance and the transcendence
of this love and care
the aeonic zeitgeist she called it
putting life in its beautiful frame
oh, the truth and its pursuit he never forsake!
He tries; She tries
He hurts, She cries
She grows, He smiles
a pair of swans in a lotus pond
oh, how delicately the two souls reunite!

14. love Me gentle

love Me gentle,

and love Me kind

for You, my heart, hold the strings to the music of my soul

15. Al-Aziz

the rose petal with dew droplets on it
the buzz of all the bees
the softness of a sparrow's feather
the glow of the gentle breeze
the warmth of the sunlight
the green of all the leaves
the meaning of every word
the essence of His Highness's existence
me, the Love in me, and the Love itself
is so full of you Al-Aziz
how is it possible for You to be so Distant
yet being so close to me

16. Untitled

it took me lovers
and a heartbroken lovee
to learn that pain demands to be felt
before it finally leaves.
for love is the most precious
divine, tender, and free
yet it cuts like a sword
and stings like a bee.
the pain wakes you up
but so does peace
then why do You want to lose it all
before You finally decide to Heal?

17. fusfus

our mystic father whispered,

as the first ray of sunlight touched my eyes,

"it is the responsibility of the one who wakes up first, to make breakfast for the other who's still asleep."

and then he said,

"be quiet when you make bread and tea, for the other shall be as restful when he wakes up, as thee."

so i whispered back to him,

"i shall not leave before the other is awake, or he shall blame you for the miracles."

and doubtedly I uttered,

"i shall leave for work, to explore the vastness of your sea, when the other is awake, for is it now his duty to prepare the tea."

and he replied,

"look around, you are already a sailor set to work, there is nowhere else to be."

and in the wetness of the tears on my cheeks, i experienced oneness with his sea.